Quebec City

Featuring the Photography of
Larry Fisher

Irving Weisdorf & Co. Ltd.

An unforgettable view of Quebec City from the St. Lawrence.

Situated at the "narrowing of the waters" (the meaning of "Kebec" in the Indian Algonquian language) Quebec is one of the most historic and beautiful cities in North America. The metropolis grew up around the confluence of the St. Charles and St. Lawrence Rivers. Here the St. Lawrence is only one kilometre wide.

When Jacques Cartier, the French explorer who claimed New France for King Francis I, came here in 1535, it was known as Stradacona, home to some 1,000 natives. More than half a century later, Cartier was followed by another French explorer, Samuel de Champlain, who set up a trading post in 1608. His statue stands out-side the Chateau Frontenac, Quebec City's most distinctive landmark.

As settlers poured in to seek their fortunes in North America, Quebec City quickly became the economic, religious and political heartbeat of New France. In the 17th and 18th centuries, it saw continuous conflict between French settlers, warring Indians and the English government. The city's location, atop 93-metre-high Cap Diamant, made it a strategic military post and a difficult place to capture. Not surprisingly, Quebec City has been dubbed the "Gibraltar of Canada." It has been besieged no fewer than six times.

Colourful night lights show off the beauty of Lower Town and the majesty of the Chateau Frontenac in Upper Town.

Quebec, a city where past and present meet to create the unique culture for which it is so famous.

(inset)
A monument to Bonhomme Carnaval, the giant snowman who presides over Quebec City's well-known winter carnival. Sometimes called the Mickey Mouse of Quebec, he represents the jovial spirit of the annual Mardi Gras festival.

A view of the city's harbour with the beauty of the St. Lawrence, the heights of Lévis and Ile d'Orleans in the background. Cruise ships often stop in Quebec's harbour as they tour the St. Lawrence.

French rule finally ended on September 13, 1759, with the Battle of the Plains of Abraham, but the inhabitants – almost half a million strong in the Greater Quebec Area – remain fiercely loyal to their francophone roots. But English traditions survive too, in such oh-so-British ceremonies such as the Changing of the Guards. Resplendent in red uniforms and black busbies, the guards go through their manoeuvres at the Citadelle, the fortress which, with the medieval-style stone wall, once formed the nucleus of the military defence system.

Each season brings a different atmosphere to Quebec City. In the summer, the provincial capital is lively with artists, street musicians and thousands of tourists who arrive by car, by plane and by cruise ship. In the fall, the streets are less crowded and the city is bathed in a symphony of orange, yellow and burgundy leaves.

The changing of the guard at the Citadelle is performed every morning by the famous Royal 22nd Regiment. It is a prime example of the military tradition and history which the city flaunts with unparalleled enthusiasm.

Two of the city's best-known landmarks stand together in the heart of Old Quebec. The Chateau Frontenac was built in 1892 on the site of the original Chateau St-Louis, prestigious home of the governors of New France. In front of the hotel stands a monument to Samuel de Champlain, who established the city in 1608.

A stroll along the historic streets of Quebec leads visitors past quaint cafes, shops and restaurants.

(next page) Beautiful at any time of the year, autumn sets this historic place ablaze with colour and sets the soul ablaze with a yearning to recapture the past.

Even in winter, Quebec City buzzes with life. Carnaval, a celebration of Mardi Gras brings thousands of visitors to town. Presided over by "Bonhomme," a giant snowman who is the festival's mascot, Carnaval is a time to forget winter chills, throw up your heels and celebrate.

Although much of Quebec City is modern, with hotels, office blocks, government buildings and soaring highrises, it is the old, walled city – divided into the Upper and Lower Towns – that has put it on the tourism map. The old city, with its narrow winding streets, historic stone buildings and castle-like hotel overlooking the St. Lawrence River, tugs at heartstrings and makes Quebec one of the most popular and romantic tourist venues in North America.

PARLIAMENT HILL

The **Parliament Building**, an imposing grey stone edifice, built in the French Renaissance style popular in France during the 16th century, is the seat of the provincial government. During the past couple of decades, it has been the scene of lively debates during the endless struggles between the federalist Liberal and Conservative parties and the separatist, Parti Quebecois.

Despite the political differences that exist between the parties, the opulent, baroque interior of the **National Assembly Chamber**, with its pale blue walls, pillars and ornate gilt woodwork, conjurs up an air of dignity and calm. The National Assembly is where the elected members of Quebec's Parliament meet. The neighbouring **Legislative Council Chamber** is where parliamentary committees get together.

Visitors can take guided tours of the 100-square metre complex with its lofty central tower. For a bird's eye view over the Parliament Building, the old walled city, the St. Lawrence River and Ile d'Orleans, go to **Anima Gallery**, an art gallery on rue de La Chevrotière. Situated on the 31st floor of the Marie-Guyart building, the tallest highrise in the city, the art gallery houses an interesting collection of local and international art.

The Parliament Building, built between 1877 and 1884, is the seat of the Quebec National Assembly. A monument to Honoré Mercier stands in front of it.

Visitors may take guided tours through the historic National Assembly Chamber (far left) and the Legislative Council Chamber, two rich and stately rooms where the ornate decor and beautiful paintings pay tribute to key figures in Quebec's history.

From political history to modern art — Quebec City has it all. One of over 50 galleries and museums in the area, Anima Gallery houses local and international work in a unique setting at the top of the tallest building in the city.

A view of Quebec's House of Parliament atop Parliament Hill, outside the walls of old Quebec.

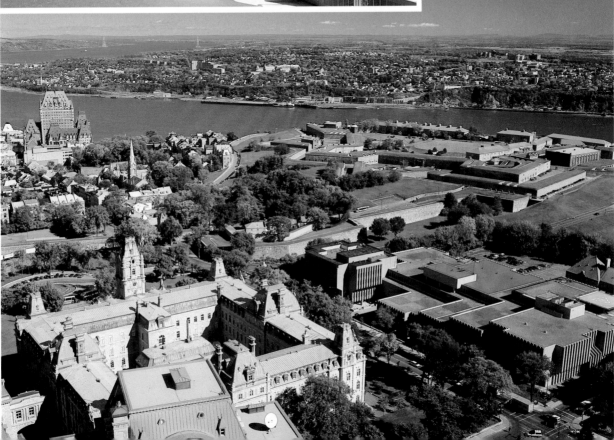

GRAND-ALLÉE

This tree-lined boulevard is often described as the "Champs Elysées" of Quebec, an apt comparison to the famous avenue in Paris, since it is lined with elegant townhouses, government buildings, statues and ritzy restaurants. It has many places of historic interest. The **Henry Stuart House**, one of the few surviving Palladian style cottages, has a rose garden and furnishings brought over from Great Britain by the family who lived there in 1849.

Also on **Grand-Allée** is a statue of the **Marquis de Montcalm**, commander of the French troops in New France, who was slain on the Plains of Abraham. The British General, James Wolfe, was also killed in the battle. A monument to Wolfe, marking the spot where he fell, stands in Battlefields Park.

A major highway in colonial times – it was used by native traders transporting their furs to the city – Grand-Allée today is one of the most prestigious places to work and live in Quebec City. At its southern end is the **Port Saint Louis**, an arched, stone opening in the wall which leads to the historic Upper Town.

Henry Stuart House is one of the few Palladian-style cottages left in the city. Dating back to 1849, the victorian cottage is now an historical site located on the prestigious Grande-Allée.

General Montcalm was the leader of the French troops who fought the British for control of Quebec in 1759. Montcalm died in battle with his British adversary, General Wolfe, on the Plains of Abraham, September 13th, 1759.

The St. Louis Gate is one of the main gateways into old Quebec. Once past the old city walls, visitors are engulfed by the city's romantic charm and fascinated by its history.

In colonial times, Grande-Allée boulevard was the main route which linked Quebec City with Cap-Rouge, where Natives of the Sillery reserve travelled to sell their furs in town. Today it is lined with colourful cafés and restaurants where visitors can find culinary delights to please any taste.

In the summer, restaurateurs and bar owners along the Grande-Allée roll up their tarpaulins and bring tables and chairs outside to officially launch "terrasse season," a summer-long celebration of warm weather, good food and good company.

Now part of Battlefields Park, the Plains of Abraham was the site of the famous battle between General Montcalm and General Wolfe for control of Quebec. It was here that the national anthem, "O Canada," was first sung on June 24, 1880. Re-enactments of the 1759 battle still take place here to show visitors how New France fell to the British. (inset) One of the four martello towers built in the 19th century.

Several points throughout the park commemorate the struggle for Quebec with plaques, monuments and artillery artifacts. It's the perfect place to take an historical journey and learn about one of the most important moments in Canadian history.

The Citadelle, located atop Cap Diamant, is the most impressive of the city's fortifications. Construction of the Citadelle began in 1820 and continued for more than 30 years. The military tradition is most clearly represented by the daily changing of the guard of the 22nd Regiment. The Royal 22nd Regiment Museum, which offers historical exhibits dating back to the 17th century, is also on the site.

BATTLEFIELDS PARK

Wandering around the **Plains of Abraham**, a lovely park with groves of trees, picnic tables and restful views over the St. Lawrence River, it is hard to imagine that it was once the scene of a bloody battle. In a skirmish that lasted a mere 20 minutes, some 4,500 British troops commanded by General James Wolfe, fought the Marquis de Montcalm and his French army, sealing the fate of New France.

The Plains of Abraham are said to have been named after Abraham Martin, a river pilot who owned the land. It's now part of Battlefields Park, a 250-acre expanse of greenery which embraces several sites commemorating the struggle for Quebec. Within the park are two **martello towers**, part of the defence system built by the British at the beginning of the 19th century.

The heart of that defense system was the **Citadelle**, a sprawling, star-shaped fort (one of several that have been built on the site) at the south east corner of the 4.5 kilometre-long wall which circles the old city. Twenty-five buildings, including an officers' mess, two military museums and the Governor-General's residence make up the complex, still a base for soldiers. The famed 22nd Regiment, popularly known as the Van Doos (a mispronunciation of vingt-deux) is headquartered here.

A pretty sunken garden designed in 1938 by landscape architect Louis Perron, commemorates the soldiers who were killed on the Plains of Abraham. In the middle stands a statue of **Joan of Arc**, mounted on a horse. Another picturesque spot is the Earl Grey Terrace (Governor-General of Canada at the beginning of the century and the same person that the tea is named after) from which you can see out over the St. Lawrence River.

Also in Battlefields Park is the **Musée du Quebec**, three buildings housing a collection of over 17,000 paintings, sculptures, silver, prints, drawings, photographs and decorative art, dating back to the early years of French settlement. The museum was renovated and expanded in 1987 when the original neoclassical building (now known as Pavilion Gerard-Morriset) was linked to an 1870 stone jail by The Great Hall, a glass-roofed structure which seems to surge out of the ground.

This monument was erected in Battlefields Park to commemorate the heroes of 1759 and 1760. With an inscription honouring the virtue and valour of Joan of Arc, it was presented to the National Battlefields Commission by two anonymous donors.

This monument stands outside the century-old Armoury building on the Grande-Allée.

The Musée du Québec stands in the heart of Battlefields Park. First opened in 1933, most of the museum is dedicated to Quebec art.

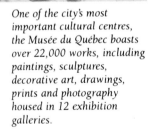

One of the city's most important cultural centres, the Musée du Québec boasts over 22,000 works, including paintings, sculptures, decorative art, drawings, prints and photography housed in 12 exhibition galleries.

The Chateau Frontenac hotel is the most famous Quebec City landmark, standing at the height of Cap Diamant.

UPPER TOWN

The old part of Quebec City, which covers 11 square kilometres, is laid out on two levels – Upper Town, which sits on top of Cap Diamant and Lower Town which huddles below it, across from the Vieux Port (Old Port) and the St. Lawrence River. In colonial times, Upper Town was the centre of political, military and religious life.

The hub of power was Chateau St-Louis, the residence of the governors of New France, including the fiery and controversial Louis de Buade, Comte de Frontenac. In defiance of orders from the French government, Frontenac set up a series of forts across North America (they ranged as far as the Great Lakes and the Mississippi) in order to further his business interests in the fur trade.

Count Frontenac died in 1698, on the brink of being dismissed from his prestigious position (his independent streak had prompted skirmishes with warring Iroquois and the British) but his name lives on in the **Chateau Frontenac**, the castle-like hotel which towers above the Upper Town. The hotel was constructed just over a century ago (it celebrated its centenary in 1993) on almost the same spot occupied by the old governmental headquarters.

One of a chain of hotels built by railway companies across Canada, the Chateau Frontenac, which is operated by Canadian Pacific Hotels and Resorts, looks like a medieval French chateau. The 650-room hostelry, with its tower, turrets and distinctive copper roof, is not only one of Quebec City's most prestigious hotels, it's also an historic landmark and major tourist attraction.

Even if you don't stay at the hotel, wander inside to take a look at the lavish interior. Chateau Frontenac is indeed as grand as a European castle. The dining areas, reception halls and meeting rooms which are embellished with pillars and carved woodwork, are decorated with antiques, oil paintings and chandeliers. Famous guests who have stayed here include royalty, prime ministers and Hollywood stars, like Queen Juliana of the Netherlands, Hailé Sélassié (Emperor of Ethiopia), Sir Winston Churchill, President Franklin Delano Roosevelt, President Charles de Gaulle, Bing Crosby, Boris Karloff and Anthony Quinn.

In front of the Chateau Frontenac runs **Dufferin Terrace**, a 670-metre long boardwalk with gazebos which

In the past this majestic hotel has hosted Queen Elizabeth and Prince Philip and many other foreign dignitaries. During World War II, Roosevelt and Churchill met at the hotel which was completely evacuated for security reasons.

The interior of the hotel is as impressive as the exterior. The ornate restored decor creates a sense of nostalgia for guests while they enjoy a luxurious and elegant setting.

The century-old hotel can be seen from nearly any place within the old city walls.

are linked by park benches. It's a pleasant place to walk or to sit and snack while enjoying the scenic views over the Lower Town and the St. Lawrence River. Even in winter, when it can get very cold on top of Cap Diamant, you'll see couples strolling arm in arm. In summer, Dufferin Terrace rings with the sounds of street musicians.

At one end of the Dufferin Terrace is a 15-metre high statue of Samuel de Champlain, who founded Quebec in 1608. Beside the statue is a monument erected by the United Nations Educational, Scientific and Cultural Organization. Quebec City was declared a UNESCO World Heritage Site in 1985, an honour which puts it on a par with the Great Barrier Reef, the Grand Canyon and the Acropolis.

A view of the Old Post Office and the Samuel de Champlain monument at night, from the Dufferin Terrace.

Visitors will be charmed by a view of Quebec City at night, especially while strolling along the Dufferin Terrace beside the Chateau Frontenac.

Quebec's famous boardwalk was first constructed around 1840 by Lord Durham, then governor of New France. It has been renovated and expanded several times over the years and was eventually named after Governor Lord Dufferin.

Across from the **UNESCO** monument is **Place d'Armes**, a former training square for soldiers and the **Musée du Fort**, where you can watch a sound and light show which explains, with gripping reality, through dioramas and special effects, the military history of Quebec. On the other side of the street is the Maison du Tourisme, the local tourist office, where visitors can get information about Quebec City and its surroundings.

The streets that fan out from Place d'Armes are lined with imposing public buildings, from the past and present. Quebec's **Hotel de Ville** (City Hall) on rue des Jardins, is the centre of the municipal government. It was built in 1896 on the site of a former Jesuit church.

The Roman Catholic church wielded great power over the political and educational life of New France. The **Seminaire de Québec** was founded in 1663, as a training centre for priests. By the 1800s, it had become the most prestigious

(top right)
The Musée du Fort offers a complete picture of Quebec's military history. Presentations illustrate the six sieges of the city, including the Battle of the Plains of Abraham, using light, sound and models.

(right)
The fountain in the centre of Place d'Armes is a monument to faith. It was erected to commemorate the tricentennial of the arrival of the Récollet missionaries in 1615.

The bronze, granite and glass UNESCO monument marks the naming of Quebec City as a World Heritage Site in 1985. It is the first North American city to be given this prestigious honour.

boys' school in Canada. Laval University, the first French-speaking university in North America, was established here in 1949.

The twin-towered **Notre-Dame Basilica** was the mother church for the religious elite who ruled over New France. The oldest cathedral in North America (it dates back over 350 years), it has a lavish, baroque interior. The chancel lamp was a gift from the Sun King himself, Louis XIV. Most of the bishops of Quebec are buried in the crypt, as is Count Frontenac.

Holy Trinity on rue des Jardins, which is modelled after London's Saint-Martin-in-the-Fields, is Quebec City's Anglican cathedral. It contains several religious objects donated by King George III.

Like many other buildings in the city, Quebec's city hall is housed in a magnificent heritage building.

A view of the St-Jean gate, one of the three remaining gates through the old city walls.

The Seminaire de Quebec was founded by Bishop Laval, Quebec's first bishop. The seminary's quiet grounds are open to public tours during the summer.

The Ursulines were a teaching order of nuns who arrived from France in 1639. A museum, which traces their lives from New France to the present day, is part of the Ursuline monastery on rue Donnacona. Montcalm is buried in the crypt of the Ursuline chapel, which is part of the monastery complex. Oddly, his skull is on display in a glass case.

The Ursuline chapel shelters the remains of General Montcalm and the tomb of Marie L'Incarnation. The copper statue is a tribute to Marie de L'Incarnation, Reverend Mother and settler of New France. She was one of the founders of the convent in 1639.

(opposite)
The Basilica of Notre Dame has endured a long history of bombardment, reconstruction and restoration, yet it remains a beautiful and powerful symbol of the strength of the Church and its role in the history of Quebec.

The Quebec Department of Tourism is located in a central part of the old city, in the old Union Hotel, built in 1805

Lined with quaint cafés and shops, rue St. Louis is one of the main streets in Upper Town.

Quebec City has always attracted artists because of its history, charm and beauty. The city's love affair with art began with the first settlers and continues today. On rue du Trésor you can buy a taste of Quebec and bring it home with you, at a reasonable price too!

The narrow streets of Quebec City are not geared to modern modes of transportation. Once there, most visitors abandon their cars and explore the town on foot. By walking, rather than driving, you can discover the alleyways and courtyards that make this city such an architectural treasure.

Along **rue du Trésor**, a narrow lane leading from rue Ste-Anne, artists sell sketches, etchings and watercolours from tiny, cheek-by-jowl street stalls. Along **rue St. Louis** is a multitude of restaurants, tucked away in old houses with thick stone walls, steep roofs and dormer windows. Quebec City has many parks like **Jardin des Gouverneurs**, the small garden that surrounds a monument commemorating Generals Wolfe and Montcalm.

Jardin des Governeurs surrounds the Wolfe-Montcalm monument, a tribute to the famous adversaries.

Exploring Upper Town on foot allows for the opportunity to find hidden architectural treasures.

The beautiful Gare du Palais, the city's train station, was designed by Bruce Price, who also designed the Chateau Frontenac.

Beautiful Quebec City has been described as a fairy-tale-type place. Aside from its rich natural beauty and charming architecture, it is the only remaining walled city in North America. Visitors need not leave the space within these walls, as there's much to see and do here. No itinerary is necessary, just the time and desire to wander about experiencing all Quebec City has to offer.

Even the military installations have been landscaped with lawns, shrubs and flowers. At Place d'Youville which leads to Port St-Jean, one of the entrances in the wall, is Artillery Park, the headquarters of the Royal Artillery Regiment who were garrisoned here in the 19th century. In this area too, is the newly renovated Théâtre Capitole, a turn-of-the-century music hall which has hosted such famous stars of yesteryear as Maurice Chevalier, Edith Piaf and Sarah Bernhardt.

When your feet get tired, jump into a **horse-drawn calèche**. Like regular taxis, they have a parking stand, across from the Château Frontenac. The drivers are a terrific source of information (they also accept credit cards!) and can advise visitors on everything from where to find a post office, to the best place to eat. Quebec City has dozens of restaurants serving everything from hearty, Quebecois fare – tourtière (meat pie), fèves aux lards (beans) and the like – to the finest French cuisine.

The Royal 22nd Regiment on parade at the Citadelle.

A ride in a calèche is a romantic way to tour Upper Town and see the sites outside the old city walls.

Each restaurant in Quebec seems to flaunt its own particular character, as does La Vieille Maison du Spaghetti (right). Not to be outdone by other restaurants, it too has an outdoor café.

Sidewalk cafés are a sure sign of summer in Quebec. Whether on main thoroughfares or tiny, hidden sidestreets, restaurateurs throughout the city mark the beginning of summer by setting up patios and serving customers outside.

Quebec is home to hundreds of bars, cafés and restaurants eager to entertain tourists from around the world. Tourists flock to Quebec City for the food as well as the sights. Restaurateurs here follow the French tradition of haute cuisine, which means food is prepared with the utmost care and service is superb.

The landmark Chateau Frontenac looks even more majestic from the lighthouse in Lower Town, at the base of Cap Diamant.

LOWER TOWN

To get to Lower Town from Upper Town, tourists can take a short ride on a **funicular railway**. This unique little train with its glass walls, gives views over Lower Town and the Vieux Port. As you descend, you can see the ferries which ply back and forth between Quebec City and Lévis, on the south shore of the St. Lawrence River. At a dollar a ride, the funicular is surely one of the cheapest and most scenic sightseeing tours anywhere.

In Lower Town, the train stops inside the **Maison Louis Jolliet**. Jolliet was the Canadian-born explorer, fur-trader and cartographer, who together with Father Marquette, discovered the Mississippi River. A plaque beside the building commemorates their journey.

While the settlement on top of Cap Diamant was the stronghold of the movers and shakers of the day, the Lower Town was home to more humble folk – settlers, fur traders and merchants who lived and worked around the bustling, narrow streets which fanned back from the river. By 1662, over 35 parcels of land had been granted to entrepreneurs who set up shop at the base of Cap Diamant.

The funicular railway is a unique way of travelling from Upper Town to Lower Town and back again, without having to tackle the steep hill and all those stairs!

Quartier Petit-Champlain is considered the oldest village in North America. Part of Lower Town Quebec, the village was once a busy port with trading posts and elegant 17th-century residences. Visitors now meander down its restored cobble-stone streets, taking in all the flavours of Quebec's past and present.

Quebec City is famous for its cliffside elevator which offers
a spectacular view of Lower Town and the St. Lawrence River.

The quaint arts and craft shops, cafés and bakeries which line the tiny
colourful streets of Lower Quebec lure visitors back again and again.

(opposite page)
The unique architecture of the Lower Town houses, with their steep-sloping roofs and dormer windows, makes Quebec's old harbour village welcoming and comforting.

If going down the aptly-named Breakneck Stairs seems scary, climbing the stairs back to Upper Town is even more daunting and in the winter, they are often more treacherous.

Rue de Petit Champlain, at the base of Casse-Cou, remains lively at night, offering visitors more time to linger in the charming old village.

Rue du Petit Champlain dates back to this era, which is why it is said to be the oldest shopping centre in North America. The lively little thoroughfare, lined with some 50 shops, art galleries, restaurants and boutiques, runs from the bottom of the **Casse-Cou** (breakneck) stairs, past the funicular station to the Boulevard Champlain.

It doesn't take long to walk from one end to the other, but you're sure to be sidetracked for an hour or two, by the eye-catching merchandise offered for sale. Souvenir shops flog the usual T-shirts and plastic ornaments but you'll also find designer suits, hand-thrown pottery, glassware, ceramic jewelry, leather bags and papier-maché masks.

La Fresque des Québécois

At night, a soft, romantic glow descends over **rue Petit Champlain**, but even late in the day, the street is lively. Many of the stores and galleries stay open until 9 p.m. or later. The restaurants are open too, along the street and up the Breakneck Stairs. Painted on a wall of the Soumande House on Place Royale in Quebec City and inaugurated on October 17, 1999, **La Fresque des Québécois** is painted in trompe-l'oeil and tells the story of Quebec's National Capital. The artists created this 420 m² fresque to depict Quebec's architecture, its geographical location, its fortification, walls, its staircases as well as its seasonal colors.

(opposite page)
Rue de Petit Champlain is considered the oldest street in North America, dating back to the founding of the city in 1608.

VIEUX PORT

One of Quebec City's most interesting museums, the **Musée de la civilisation** is, like so many others in this handsome old town, housed in historic buildings. Situated in the heart of the Vieux Port, the museum is actually three buildings in one, blended together with a new facade, designed by Israeli-Canadian architect Moshe Safdie.

Safdie's distinctive touch (he also designed Montreal's innovative Habitat built for EXPO 67 and the National Gallery in Ottawa) is evident in the museum's ultra-modern design. Fashioned from grey limestone, the building, which opened in 1988, is topped by a green, glass tower, whose shape echoes the spires of the historic churches that grace the skyline of the old city.

In the lobby of the museum is a large, angular sculpture entitled "La Debacle" (a reference to the breaking up of ice in the spring) by Montreal artist Astri Reusch. From there, a stairway leads visitors through exhibition halls where displays are organized into themes: "Memoires," "Objets de Civilization," "La Barque" and "Messages."

A wide variety of artifacts are on display – metal coats of armor, ornately decorated carriages, simple folk art and Quebecois furniture. The wooden armoires (large cupboards) with diamond designs on the doors, so common in 18th and 19th centuries, have now become collectors' pieces.

Astri Reusch's "La Débâcle," a reinforced concrete sculpture residing in a shallow pool, greets visitors in the large entrance hall to the Musée de la civilisation.

The modern Musée de la civilisation lies in the heart of old Quebec, near Place-Royale and Vieux Port. The museum's impressive architectural design has been recognized for its integration into the traditional architecture of Old Quebec.

The museum's large collection of wood-work pays tribute to carpentry and furniture making which were important crafts in early Quebec culture.

Exhibits of early Quebec folk art record the history, culture and way of life of the earliest settlers.

(above left)
This elaborate carriage is part of the "Memoires" exhibit at the Musée de la civilisation.

This life-size metal statue was part of Les Hommes de Fer D'Autriche Impériale, an exhibit held at the museum in 1995. It included treasures of art, arms and armour from Imperial Austria, used by knights from the 15th and 17th centuries.

The Louis Jolliet offers daily cruises on the St. Lawrence, leaving from the Chouinard Pier in Lower Quebec. Visitors will find the view of the city skyline from the river unforgettable.

The Vieux Port Centre d'Interpretation provides yet another journey into Quebec's heritage through historical exhibits on industry and trade.

The restored Vieux Port has now become a major tourist attraction but in the 19th century it was an important centre for industrial and commercial activity.

A spectacular view of Quebec's harbour and Lévis at night.

Across from Musée de la civilisation is the pier from which Louis Jolliet, a sightseeing boat, sets off for trips around the harbour. The ship, which is named after the man who helped to discover the Mississippi, plies the St. Lawrence River three times a day. The guided tour takes passengers past Quebec City's spectacular skyline then turns towards Ile d'Orleans, past the Montmorency Falls.

In days gone by, the Vieux Port was the gateway to the province and the rest of Canada. As recently as the 19th century, there were no proper roads to the interior and the St. Lawrence River was the "highway" along which merchandise – furs, lumber and other raw materials – was transported to the outside world.

The Vieux Port is an 82-acre complex of warehouses, docks, grain elevators and a yacht marina which winds around the mouth of the St. Charles River where it joins the St. Lawrence. At one time, the St. Lawrence came right up to the row of buildings along rue Dalhousie. Expansions through the decades, created by landfill, have pushed the Vieux Port further out into the water.

When planes replaced ships and trains as the major forms of transportation, the Vieux Port fell into disrepair. In recent years, however, the federal govenment has poured millions of dollars into creating what is now one of Quebec's major tourist attractions, with musicians, restaurants, street performers and dozens of cruise ships, which call here during the summer and fall.

The Vieux Port Centre d'Intrepretation on rue Saint-André gives a good overview of the past. Exhibits trace the history of Quebec's lumber and shipbuilding industries. In the early 1800s, before steel and steam overtook wood and sail, local shipyards turned out over 2,500 vessels.

(next page)
The jovial spirit of the city cannot be quelled, even in winter. The annual winter Carnaval delights tourists and residents alike, offering them a chance to kick up their heels and have some good, cold winter fun.

CARNAVAL

In the winter, Quebec City has a particularly romantic atmosphere. Bathed in snow and garlanded with ice, the old buildings take on the look of a Dickensian Christmas card. Even during the coldest season, visitors flock into town – especially during the annual Carnaval, a celebration of Mardi Gras.

During Carnaval, which is held in early February, the streets of the city erupt in a wild profusion of colour and sound. The round of revelry goes on for 11 days, as over half a million people pour into town to have fun and enjoy the street parades, hockey matches, dances and ice sculpting competitions, which are part of the festivities.

Bonhomme Carnaval, a giant snowman clad in a red toque and sash, presides over the proceedings with relentless goodwill. His jolly persona and patter set the tone and the pace for the winter streetfest. To preserve the mystique of Carnaval, Bonhomme's identity is never revealed, but his smiling face is seen everywhere – on posters, T-shirts and keyrings. Bonhomme is a shrewd marketing concept, but somehow he's more than a mere symbol. The snowman is the spirit of fantasy and fun that makes this festival one of the liveliest in North America.

Carnaval kicks off with the crowning of a Carnaval Queen at **Bonhomme's Snow Palace**, an extravagant creation 41 metres long, 23 metres wide and 48 metres high, which is built into the city wall on Dufferin Avenue, opposite the Parliament building.

In former years, the Snow Palace was constructed from ice, but it cost over $30,000 to build, much too expensive for a structure with such a short life span. These days, snow is trucked in from the St. Charles River.

The snow-covered streets of Quartier Petit Champlain are charming even on a cold winter night.

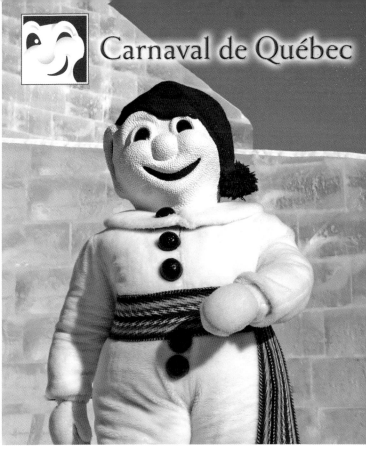

Bonhomme's Snow Palace. This life-size majestic castle is built every year specifically for Carnaval. A wonder to see, this huge snow sculpture is the site of many shows and activities throughout the 11-day celebration. (inset) Images of the jolly snowman mascot are everywhere during Carnaval. This illuminated Bonhomme is at the top of the Snow Palace.

Children and adults alike are delighted when Bonhomme shows his smiling face, a character second only to Santa Claus in popularity here.

The Quebec sense of "joie de vivre" takes shape in many forms, including this peculiar tradition of revelling in the snow with nearly nothing on.

(next page)
It's worth the short trip east of the city to see Montmorency Falls. The site of the falls is divided into upper and lower sections with lookout points, hiking trails, picnic grounds and historic sites.

AROUND QUEBEC CITY

When Samuel de Champlain sailed up the St. Lawrence River in 1603, he noted in his journal "a torrent of water falling over the top of a great mountain." As was the custom in New France, he named the landmark after a prominent figure of the time. The "torrent of water," became Montmorency Falls, a reference to Admiral Henri de Montmorency, Viceroy of New France.

Montmorency Falls continues to impress visitors — not least because this spectacular display of nature plunges earthwards for 84 metres, 30 metres more than the mighty Niagara Falls. The falls were harnessed as far back as 1885 when Quebec City became the first community in Canada to utilize hydro-electric power.

The force of the water has sculpted a huge pond at the foot of the falls and during the winter, when most of the water freezes, a cone of snow and ice emerges from the middle. The "Pain du Sucre" (sugarloaf), as locals call it and the partly frozen falls, provide a playground for sledders, skiers and ice-climbers.

Not far from Montmorency Falls is the bridge to Ile d'Orleans, named for another prominent historical figure, the Duke of Orleans.

(opposite page)
Montmorency Falls is an amazing sight to behold in the winter. Its spray, frozen by the cold, creates a beautiful natural wonder and a great place for tobogganing.

The town of Gaspé seems to have been untouched by the modern century. It remains a rural pocket of land where Quebec heritage and culture is preserved in the heart of the people.

The Percé Rock juts out of the Gulf of the St. Lawrence near the Gaspé Peninsula. This remarkable rock formation is 510 metres long and 100 metres wide with an average height of 70 metres.

Ile d'Orleans, which is only 67 kilometres in circumference, retains the ambience of the past. Many of the families who live here can trace their heritage back to the pioneers who came from Normandy and Brittany, following the explorations of Samuel de Champlain. Many vestiges of New France remain – old farmhouses, seigneurial "manoirs" and steep-roofed, dormer-windowed homes with thick, stone walls.

The historic atmosphere is created by the rural countryside and by the large number of old buildings. The rolling farmland, interspersed with sleepy hamlets such as St-Pierre, Ste-Famille and St-Laurent, each dominated by a typically Quebecois, silver-spired church, also evokes the feeling of a bygone era.

The north-east tip of Ile d'Orleans offers a great view of Mont Ste-Anne, an 823-metre high mountain which is surrounded by a recreational park. One of the most popular ski centres in Eastern North America, for both cross country and alpine skiing (snowboarding is also popular here), Mont Ste-Anne has a sophisticated snowmaking system which covers 85 per cent of its 50 trails giving the resort a longer winter season than most.

Ile d'Orleans is a treasure-chest of century-old houses, mills and churches, including this typical Quebecois church in Ste-Pierre (above) and the brightly-coloured Ste-Famille church, built in 1748 (below).

*L'Ile aux Coudres,
near Charlevoix,
has a rich maritime
history and has
many treasures of
the past, including
this ship-wrecked
fishing boat.*

*The maritime tradition in St. Laurent goes back to its
founding in 1679. In fact, boats were the main means of
transportation here until 1935. The modern marina is the
only one on Ile d'Orleans and can accommodate 130 boats.*

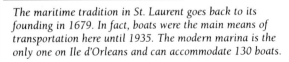

*Like many other churches on the island, the church in
St. Laurent is more than a century old, dating back to 1860.*

*(next page)
Baie St. Paul is a small community at the mouth of the
Gouffre River, near Charlevoix, east of Quebec City.*

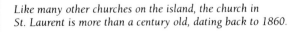

Mont Ste-Anne's 215-kilometres of cross country trails and its sophisticated lift system makes it one of the leading ski centres in the province. Every hour, a network of gondolas and chairlifts hoist almost 18,000 skiers to the peak. Even if you don't ski, it's well worth taking a trip to the top. The panoramic view, over the Beaupré coast and the St. Lawrence River, is spectacular.

Mont Ste-Anne is the largest ski resort in all of Quebec and attracts thousands of skiers of all skill-levels every year.

With over 40 challenging runs, Mont Ste-Anne's are said to be the best groomed ski trails in North America.

Thrill-seekers will love skiing on Mont Ste-Anne's more challenging runs, some of which are certified by the International Ski Federation.

Mont Ste-Anne's eight-passenger gondola brings skiers to the top of the mountain in less than eight minutes.

The view from Mont Ste-Anne is breathtaking, especially from the south face, the highest of the summit's three faces.

Mont Ste-Anne also attracts outdoor lovers during the summer months. The area offers a myriad of sporting activities – golf (there are two 18-hole courses), in-line skating, mountain biking, para-gliding and hiking. Near the park is Chutes Ste-Anne, a 74-metre-high waterfall, which tumbles down a series of natural stone steps, into a spectacular canyon. Lookout points and a bridge, 55-metres above the water, lead visitors around the scenic gorge.

A parachuting school offers lessons year-round from the top of the mountain. It's a safe bet you will never forget this unique Mont Ste-Anne experience.

As beautiful in the summer as in winter, Mont Ste-Anne offers avid golfers two spectacular courses at the base of the mountain.

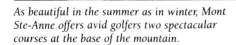

A variety of sports are popular at the Mont Ste-Anne resort during the summer. Try the challenging three kilometre paved trail at the base of the mountain.

The hiking trails, picnic grounds and camping facilities at Mont Ste-Anne is perfect for family vacations, quiet getaways and nature walks.

Built in Neo-Roman style, the architectural design of the basilica is admired for its ornate columns, vaulted ceilings and awe-inspiring stained glass windows.

(opposite page)
As breathtaking as Montmorency Falls, the Ste-Anne Falls is surrounded by some of the most beautiful scenery in Quebec and steeped in Quebec folklore. Legend has it that long ago, two lovers leapt to their deaths into the falls because they could not be together.

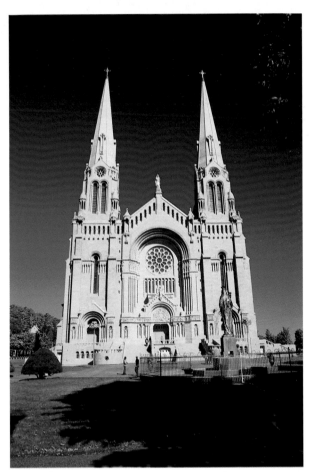

Over one-and-a-half million people make a pilgrimage to Ste-Anne de Beaupré Basilica each year. The modern church, built in 1923, stands on the site of an original wooden chapel dedicated to Saint Anne as early as 1658. A place of miracles, the sick and the lame are said to be healed when they visit this place and, according to local beliefs, Saint Anne saved many ship-wreck victims off Cap Tourmente in the 17th and 18th centuries.

Six kilometres south of the waterfall is one of Quebec's most important religious sites – **Ste-Anne de Beaupré**. The neo-Roman basilica with its twin towers, dates back to only 1923 but it is the fifth church to be built by the shores of the St. Lawrence River. The community of Ste-Anne has been a religious site since 1658, when it's believed that Ste-Anne, mother of the Virgin Mary, saved the lives of sailors shipwrecked off nearby Cap Tourmente.

The present church, which is built of sparkling silver granite, attracts almost two million pilgrims a year, who come here for healing and to pay homage to one of Quebec's most popular saints. The interior, with its arched pillars, is decorated with mosaics and beautiful, stained glass windows.

East of Ste-Anne, further down the St. Lawrence River, is the mountainous region of Charlevoix, sometimes dubbed the "Switzerland of Quebec." Named after a Jesuit priest, Francois Xavier de Charlevoix, who travelled the area in 1719, it is one of the province's most beautiful regions. Villages sprawl across valleys and around mountains. Fields are carpeted with wild flowers. Roads, rise and fall, as they follow the contours of the land.

The scenic surroundings have bred a vibrant, cultural community. Charlevoix is home to dozens of artists, writers, potters, weavers, musicians and photographers. Baie St-Paul, one of the region's biggest towns, has more than 20 art galleries, displaying the works of painters from around the region.

Among the most common subjects for painters – apart from the landscape – are the goélettes, wooden boats which were once the mainstay of the local economy. The hardy little cargo vessels carried lumber from the north, fruit and vegetables from the south, before the roads were built. Their weathered hulls lie, like beached whales, around the shores of Ile aux Coudres, an island which is also part of Charlevoix.

Scenic, romantic and steeped in history – words that aptly describe Quebec City and the region which surrounds it. The city was the heart of New France and while Quebeckers have long since joined the modern world, strong traces of the past remain, in the cultural institutions, in the language and in the architecture of this unique corner of Canada.

Quebeckers' tenacity and pride in their past is the root of the nationalism which is part of the province's political life today. For visitors, however, it is the welcoming spirit of joie de vivre and the warmth of the locals, that make Quebec City, such a popular place for a vacation.

The pioneers who followed on the heels of Jacques Cartier and Samuel de Champlain, led a life often filled with hardship and poverty and the kinds of problems unimaginable to modern man. Despite the hard times, a love of life and pride in their francophone roots has survived, richly mixed with the culture of the native peoples and immigrants from around the world, who also make their home in this fascinating part of North America.

Contents

Published and Distributed by
Irving Weisdorf & Co. Ltd.
2801 John Street,
Markham, Ontario, L3R 2Y8

Editor	Writer	Photo Researcher	Designer
Sandra Tonn	**Helga Loverseed**	**Hilary Forrest**	**Jack Steiner**

Photographs by Larry Fisher

Comstock
E. Otto — 51b
E. Sorilla — 51a

Gerard Romany — 4b, 30/31, 37a, 44/45, 46, 47b,c, 60a, 61a,b,f

Irving Weisdorf & Co. Ltd. — 8b, 22c, 26b, 29a, 29b, 32a,d, 34a,c, 61d

J.-F. Bergeron / Enviro Foto — 5c, 11a,b,c, 32b,c, 36

Masterfile
S. Hines — 6/7

Nino H. Photography — 4a, 16/17

Robert Chiasson — 18

Tony Stone
J. Edwards — 38, 50

The following photos courtesy of:

Canadian Pacific Hotels and Resorts — 20c
La Salle de l'Assemblée nationale/
    Claude Bureau — 8a
La Salle du Conseil législatif/
    Bernard Vallée — 9a
Mont Sainte-Anne — 56, 57
Musée du Québec — 15c,d,
Musée de la civilisation — 40a
    Pierre Soulard — 41